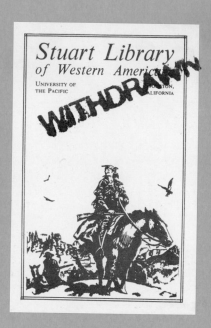

PHOTOGRAPHER OF A FRONTIER
the photographs of Peter Britt

About the Author. Alan Clark Miller's interest in the life and photographs of Peter Britt began during his boyhood in Grants Pass, Oregon, a town just a few miles north of the fading mining camp of Jacksonville. As interest in the past revived Jacksonville, Miller became intrigued with the unique tale which Peter Britt had left in the form of pictures of the first settlers, miners and farmers to settle the scenic Rogue and Applegate river valleys. Then, following his Bachelor's degree from Dartmouth and while attending Trinity College, Miller chose Britt as the subject for his Master's thesis. Cloistered in the collection of the Jacksonville Museum, he uncovered a priceless legacy of the life and times of a small community on the western frontier. It was all preserved: the diaries, reports, journals, letters from townspeople to those left on the East Coast or Midwestern Plains, and thousands upon thousands of glass plates, paper prints, rare daguerreotypes, and ambrotypes. In piecing together the story, Alan Miller has brought Peter Britt and Jacksonville to life.

Interface
Monographs on
Photography:

Fine California
Views:
The Photographs of
A. W. Ericson

With Nature's
Children:
Emma B. Freeman,
Camera and Brush

Interface
California Corporation
Eureka

PHOTOGRAPHER OF A FRONTIER

the photographs of Peter Britt

by ALAN CLARK MILLER

To

Frances Miller
   my wife
and Alvin and Eileen Miller
   my parents

The author wishes to thank the many persons who have aided him in the preparation of this monograph. There are many individuals who, through their active participation, deserve individual mention. Among these are the reference librarians and archivists without whom this research could not have been accomplished. Specific mention is due Mrs. Edna Mae Hill, Mrs. Lois Hardy, Mr. Richard Portal and Mr. Peter Knapp.

The surviving members of the Britt family were very helpful. I especially thank Mrs. Mabel Britt Riedemann of Greenville, Illinois and Mrs. Esther Britt Deichmann of Ladonia, Missouri for their valuable assistance. Mrs. H. W. Funke of Grants Pass, Oregon deserves special recognition for her translations of many virtually illegible letters and documents. Dr. Edward W. Sloan and Dr. Glenn Weaver were most helpful in their suggestions and criticisms. In addition, I express special thanks to Mr. C. William Burke and the staff of the Jacksonville Museum.

Many individuals have aided in the preparation of the manuscript. Among these, the author thanks Mr. Peter Palmquist for his extensive contribution in selecting the images for the portfolio, preparing reproduction prints and providing important commentary regarding the processes and methods that Peter Britt employed. I also wish to thank Sidney Dominitz, Robert J. Dolezal and the staff of Interface California Corporation for the aid that they gave in preparing the manuscript for publication.

Table of Contents

Peter Britt
1819-1905

Introduction

In western Oregon, a popular stereotype of the pioneer American was that of the rough-hewn, self-reliant individualist, taming the Pacific forests with the sweat of his brow and strength of his hands. While it is true that many such men existed in the Oregon Territory of the 1850's, many others had been drawn from all walks of life by the promise of free land and easy wealth from gold. In the ranks of the Oregon trailblazers were many perceptive, eloquent men. Along the muddy gold rush streams of southern Oregon, lawyers from Virginia and doctors from France toiled beside Massachusetts sailors, Kentucky farmers and Swiss immigrants.

Preparation of my Masters' thesis led me to the Southern Oregon Historical Society and the Jacksonville Museum. It was while I was within the wealth of their collections that I became fascinated with the story of Peter Britt.

While the deeds and names of most of the pioneers of Oregon have been relegated to dusty ledgers, Peter Britt remained a vital part of Jacksonville's life. He had been perpetuated in the names of streets, buildings and music festivals, as well as in the vast array of photographic prints held as treasured heirlooms by the members of many families.

Yet, despite his notoriety, no person had conducted a systematic research of Britt's fascinating life. In a short time, he provided clues to a clearer view of life in the frontier Pacific Northwest.

To many, the Oregon of the pioneers was a vast Hollywood motion picture setting, filled with shoot-outs, littered with desperados and overshadowed by the menace of hostile Indians. Sometimes even respected sources painted a picture more fitting of the "Tombstone Territory" than the Cascades and Pacific Northwest.

Peter Britt's legacy of photographs dispell these distortions. Captured on film were townspeople like those in any community. The colorful lives of most of the miners were revealed as they truly were — filled with hard work, long hours and meager pay. Britt's life was as interesting to those seeking insight into Nineteenth Century European immigration as to those concerned with Americana and the West.

Many problems confront the historian writing on Peter Britt. First, there is the extensive collection of camera equipment, glass negatives and memorabilia housed in the Jacksonville Museum. No researcher lacking a background in the technical aspects of early photography can properly appreciate this collection as a source of historical information without first becoming acquainted with the significance of these artifacts. Moreover, it would be difficult to gauge the value of the total collection of imagery without a knowledge of southern Oregon, its history, people and geography.

The Britt research was complicated by the significant periods of time that he spent in Obstalden, Switzerland; Highland, Illinois and Jacksonville, Oregon. To further complicate progress, many Britt documents are written in a rare German-Swiss script that makes interpretation difficult. Pieces of his story lay scattered throughout two continents and many institutions. Among these latter, the Bancroft Library, George Eastman House, Oregon Historical Society, Oregon State Archives and University of Oregon Library were especially rich in data.

The challenge implicit in my research was responsible, in great part, for the final text. Many months were spent on the project of unraveling Peter Britt's life, and further work remains to be accomplished.

The story of Peter Britt, as I have related it in this volume, depended for its accuracy upon the knowledge and aid of many individuals. I have expressed my thanks to these in the acknowledgements. Without their aid, the story of Peter Britt would have remained obscure.

Peter Britt richly deserves a place with the great photographers of the frontier West. In this, he is not alone. Many regional photographers only recently have been drawn to public attention. In each instance, a new facet of American history and many important details of frontier life have been revealed. Many others remain to be discovered.

In many areas of the country, individual researchers and scholars continue their hunt into the origins of our country. Oftentimes, they are drawn to striking photographs that reveal more clearly than written words the everyday life of the period.

For many years, a handful of photographers have been venerated beyond their unique contributions to the art and craft which they once practiced. This, unfortunately, overshadowed other worthy craftsmen.

The major institutions have begun to aid scholars in their search. At the forefront of this movement is the George Eastman House in Rochester, New York. Close behind are several major museums and prominent historical societies. With continued support, a truer picture of the origin of photography in the United States will be brought to light.

Alan Clark Miller
Plattsburgh, New York

Peter Britt: A Biography

From rowdy mining camps to the majesty of the first pictures ever taken of Crater Lake, the tireless lens of Peter Britt captured the history of Oregon and the Pacific Northwest for more than half a century. In a career that lasted from his arrival in 1852 in the boisterous mining camp town of Jacksonville, until his death more than 50 years later, Britt recorded the birth and transformation of one of America's last frontiers.

Year after year, he methodically traced a graphic history of the rugged southern Oregon frontier, a mountainous region bounded by the Pacific Ocean and what once was known as the Great American Desert. It had remained unpopulated by whites until 1850.

Britt was one of the area's first settlers and ceaselessly took pictures of his remote locale for five decades. Yet when he retired into well-heeled respectability after the turn of the century, he had also been, by turns, miner, mule train packer, bee-keeper, financier, property magnate, government meteorologist, first vintner in the Oregon Territory and a father of the region's fruit industry. The same tall, determined man who had called himself an "artist" in the 1855 census was signing "capitalist" after his name in the electoral rolls of 1902.

His was an almost classic American success story. An immigrant from Switzerland, he began his life in the United States by scouring the Illinois countryside for commissions to paint portraits. Economic hardship made him forsake that career after a few short years, and he mastered the growing art of photography less than a decade after Louis Daguerre announced his process in 1839 for rendering light into fixed images. Then, after a harrowing trip from the Midwest to the Pacific, partly on foot, Britt settled in Jacksonville, the mining camp to which he found his way in the year of its founding, 1852.

It was there, for the next 53 years, that he maintained his photographic studio. He strove to keep pace with the rapid technical and style changes in his medium, an amazing feat considering his remote location. He advanced from mirror-surfaced daguerreotypes and pictures on glass, called ambrotypes, to "wet-plate" paper photos; from tintypes to stereographs and tannin dry plates. More importantly, his camera captured a vivid and intimate account of a burgeoning American region.

Peter Britt in an early wet-plate print

17

Here were the miners beside their sluice boxes, the new frame farmhouses, the proud merchants, the hook and ladder brigade. He captured the pack trains, the stagecoach, the first locomotive in Oregon's Rogue River Valley.

His camera chronicled the social events: the feminist lecturer from Portland, the touring actors from San Francisco, footraces, Fourth of July picnics, weddings, hangings, christenings and funerals.

In his gallery were portraits of German brewers, French hoteliers, Italian peddlers, Chinese miners, Mexican muleteers, cavalry officers and Native Americans.

Frozen on metal and glass plates and preserved today in the Jacksonville Museum is a priceless legacy, thousands of views depicting the evolution of life in one Western community.

The name of Peter Britt is still a household word in southern Oregon, where each year a Peter Britt Music Festival and a Britt Antique Show are held. A Britt Avenue in southern Oregon's Medford and a Britt Student Union at Southern Oregon College commemorate Oregon's great photographer.

But his lifework has come to mean more than a small slice of provincial immortality, for it represents the equal struggles of the settler of the American West and the pioneer in the infant profession of photography.

An anecdote that mirrors both of these difficulties was one which Britt often told to friends as his most frightening experience, both as a photographer and as a resident of Jacksonville.

One day a man who had the deserved reputation of being the meanest cutthroat in the mining camp swaggered into Britt's studio, demanding a daguerreotype and posing with his pistol prominently displayed. Britt captured his menace in a marvelous shot, and his swarthy subject seemed pleased to discover himself so handsomely portrayed. He was back the next morning, however, drunk and surly. Brandishing his gun, he demanded his money back. Suprised that Britt meekly complied, he pocketed his cash, paused, laughed crazily, and then lurched out the door onto California Street and shot the first man he saw. He ended his day at the end of a rope — and Britt later learned that the gunslinger had vowed to "get me a man for breakfast."

As with so many immigrants and pioneers, the combination of a venturesome spirit and the reality of economic-religious hardship impelled Peter Britt onto the long road from the rugged mountains and fertile valleys of Switzerland to the similar grandeur of southern Oregon.

The son of a farmer, Britt grew up under the almost feudal Swiss Confederation that was resurrected after Napoleon's defeat at Waterloo. His family was Calvinist in a community where Jesuits provided the dominant political and theological force. His

The Oregon Territory, while not the dramatic land of Hollywood, was peopled with tough, short-tempered men

tiny hamlet, Obstalden, was in a poor, mountainous region with a rapidly expanding population. Jobs were scarce. This was particularly true for Peter, who — somewhat to the dismay of his family — had become a struggling painter after training in the local schools.

In time, the family succumbed to a combination of the same wanderlust and need described in the popular novel *Swiss Family Robinson*. Britt's older brother, Kaspar, had found little success as a Calvinist preacher, and Peter's mother had died in 1844. The following year his father, now almost 70 years old, became enamoured with the idea of immigration to the United States, where a sympathetic government had adopted liberal land policies allowing foreigners to acquire land with little difficulty.

Britt, then 26, traveled by wagon and riverboat with his family to Le Havre, France, then embarked for New Orleans, enroute to the mushrooming Swiss colony in Madison County, Illinois. Two months after leaving Obstalden, they had purchased a farm of 120 acres on the outskirts of the town of Highland.

Britt took up his career in art where he had left it in Switzerland, seeking portrait commissions. The most notable example done during his early days in America was his painting of the legendary soldier and Indian trader, Colonel George Davenport. The painting hangs today in the Municipal Art Museum of Davenport, Iowa.

But work generally was hard to come by for an itinerant portraitist, as were materials. Britt was forced to weave the fibers of his family's flax crop to make canvas, pound minerals to make colors, and mix his own oils and pigments.

Even more troublesome for Britt as he plied the Mississippi, making just enough from commissions to pay for his own food and lodging, was the competition posed by early photographers, or "Daguerrean artists," individuals who were already traversing the Midwestern countryside just two years after Daguerre's invention.

Britt, resourcefully deciding to join what he couldn't beat, apprenticed himself to the pre-eminent St. Louis daguerrean, J. H. Fitzgibbon. Fitzgibbon was indefatigable in seeking to advance his fledgling profession and bring it dignity. He later became president of the Photographers Association of America, and had grasped that Americans had an insatiable curiosity to see what their country and fellow citizens looked like. He imbued Britt with this idea while his training continued for most of 1847.

In the same year, Britt left to open his own studio in Highland, Illinois. Though he stayed there for some five years, only a half-dozen pictures have survived from his first days as an independent photographer, all marked "Highland, 1847." But the time marked Britt's conversion to professional status, for he sold his interest in the family farm to concentrate entirely on photography.

Walensee Lake near Peter Britt's birthplace in Obstalden, Switzerland

At the same time Britt was learning his new trade, gold fever was sweeping the Midwest. Wagon trains formed overnight throughout the Mississippi Valley following President James Polk's formal announcement of the California gold strike in December, 1848.

The great success of Britt's Highland studio probably was the force that kept the normally adventurous Britt from becoming one of the drove of Forty-niners. He stayed on in Highland, weathering a cholera epidemic that claimed some of his relatives and then endured the loss of his father, who had fought for Napoleon with the Swiss contingent at Waterloo. He also waited out the two-year probationary period needed to become an American citizen.

Highland, Illinois

Finally, in the spring of 1852, Britt sold his gallery and joined three other Swiss fortune-hunters on their way west. At 33, he was the oldest of the party, and was designated the leader on what was to become a half-year journey along the Oregon Trail. Three men rode on horseback and the fourth drove a wagon on which nestled 300 pounds of fragile and valuable camera equipment, as well as their supplies.

The Oregon Trail began at St. Joseph on the Missouri River, crossed the grassy plains and followed the Platte River to Fort Laramie, 600 miles away. The next leg of the trip would take the men over the Rocky Mountains. Not far out of Fort Laramie, the four Swiss were surrounded by a band of Sioux Indians. The others wanted to go down fighting, but Britt persuaded them to wait. When some of the Sioux galloped up to the wagon and spread a blanket, Britt threw in some hardtack and the raiders rode away.

Bearing northwest, the quartet entered the South Pass, a wind gap 7,500 feet above sea level, which was the only real opening in the Rockies. They passed the bleached skeletons of horses and lonely markers of shallow graves on the 450-mile stretch of broken terrain to Fort Bridger.

The men pushed westward, eventually following the Snake River into the Grande Ronde Valley, where they stopped for several days. But there, in the shadow of the Blue Mountains, a row that had been brewing among the four men came to a head.

The two youngest men had been impatient with the group's slow progress and wanted to travel lighter and faster. Eventually, they came to a strange arrangement. Not only did they split the party in half, but they did the same thing to their heavy wagon. Each twosome now had its own light two-wheeled cart.

They still journeyed together by foot and cart for 350 miles across the Blue Mountains and along the Umatilla River to the Columbia River. But there they parted, the younger two beating Britt and his companion to Portland by taking the water route and covering the distance from the Oregon Dalles in less than 24 hours.

After a grueling six-month haul to the west, Britt discovered to his chagrin that he did not like Portland. His friends were impressed with the growing port at the mouth of the Willamette River, but Britt saw little future there for his artistry. More exciting to him were reports from the southwest corner of the Oregon Territory. A gold strike had been made in the Rogue River Valley, and a mining town known as Table Rock City (later called Jacksonville) had sprung up.

Britt was certain that he could do well in a place where gold was said to grow on bushes, and he walked the 300 miles to Jacksonville alone. He arrived there on a brisk November morning in 1852 with his only possessions: an odd two-wheeled cart laden with camera equipment, a yoke of oxen, a mule, and five dollars in cash.

When Britt arrived, Jacksonville was a gold rush boom town of perhaps 1,500 people that had followed the pattern of mining frontier settlement. Perhaps 50 mining villages had sprung up in the isolated region between the Willamette Valley of Oregon and California's Sacramento Valley as the Forty-Niners moved northward in their quest for gold.

Within two decades, 90 percent of the camps had vanished. But Jacksonville survived because it was at the edge of a fertile agricultural basin, rimmed by thick Douglas fir. Simultaneously with the flood of California miners had come a southward migration of Oregon farmers. This agricultural element provided an essential sense of stability to the otherwise transient and rough-hewn gold rush town.

Jacksonville, Oregon (above) and Peter Britt's first home and photographic gallery

Britt fell in love with the Rogue River country instantly. He camped that first day on a brushy hillside where he later would build a succession of homes. There, in the shadow of towering firs and the white and cylindrical sentinel of Mount McLoughlin, he spent his first weeks constructing a dugout log cabin. Southern Oregon's first permanent Daguerrean gallery was in business, with its first customers the soldiers of fortune who were eager to send their "shadows" back East.

Their tales soon infected Britt with gold fever, and he padlocked his studio to take a claim on Anderson Creek. Along with several others, equally inexperienced, he built sluice boxes and worked frantically for a week — to no avail, despite the handsome yields both up and downstream from their site.

The amateur miners soon gave up in disgust — Britt's net yield was 75 cents. They only discovered later that they had built their sluice boxes with a glaring fault, allowing the gold to wash right through the contraption rather than settle and form deposits.

Cured, Britt returned to Jacksonville to find gold in his camera instead. But again he was diverted, this time by the harsh winter of 1852-53. The bad weather isolated the miners, who ran out of both beef and gunpowder. Hungry, they chased deer over the snow trying to bag their prey with hammers.

After a winter in which salt was traded for equal weights of gold, Britt and others concluded that the town needed constant supply lines. In February, 1853, a supply trail was blazed to the week-old port of Crescent City, California.

This not only assured supply sources for the miners but also eliminated forever the Rogue Valley's dependence on the commercial empire of Portland. No longer did the area dangle at the end of a 325-mile pack trail north. Jacksonville merchants could now deal via ship with the manufacturers in the San Francisco Bay area.

Britt was one of the first to outfit a pack train for the new route. It frequently took him 19 days to cover the 120 miles along the Cold Spring Mountain Trail leading a string of 26 mules, each carrying 200 pounds of supplies.

Packing became a lucrative business and some 20 to 30 trains with as many as 75 mules plied between Jacksonville and Crescent City. But the rigors of the business — up to 10 feet of snow would cover the mountain trail in winter and sole packers became prime targets of the hostile Rogue Indians — prompted Britt to sell his pack train and return to photography. His personal wealth, however, had increased from $280 in 1854 to $5,000 in 1857.

His attention also turned to altering radically the square, white frame house he had built a few yards in front of his original log cabin, a structure which had been considered adequate only during Jacksonville's first few years as a gold camp of tents and rough log buildings. The frame house was built in 1854, but by 1859 Britt was transforming it into what may have been Oregon's first example of the "Cottage Gothic" style, a craze which swept rural western homes for decades.

He stripped away the revival cornice and other classic details, replacing them with decorative masking known as "gingerbread." He placed interlacing bargeboards under the gables, decorated the windows with delicate label moldings, refinished the interior with dark, heavy woodwork, paneled wainscot and arched doorways, and added a latticed, post-supported veranda enclosed by a balustrade of lacy gothic tracery.

Mrs. Amalia Britt

The work was not long finished when Britt received a letter from his brother in Illinois, informing him that Peter's former sweetheart, a young woman named Amalia, had been widowed and left with a young son. Britt wrote to Amalia immediately, enclosing enough money for her either to return to Switzerland or, if she chose, to come to Oregon. She and her son Jake traveled down the Mississippi and around the Horn to San Francisco, by steamer to Crescent City and then by stagecoach to Applegate — where, in 1861, she and Peter were wed. A year later, a son named

Emil was born. To mark the event, Britt planted a seedling redwood. Today it still stands on the site of the Britt home, 160 feet high and 18 feet around. A daughter, Amalia, was born in 1865.

Britt again enlarged his Gothic cottage, building a second story for his photographic business, installing a wine cellar, studio and solarium. He added dormer windows with curvilinear bargeboards and gothic finials, as well as cedar eave troughs with scalloped trim. His finishing touch was a distinctive coat of pumpkin-colored paint.

As a cameraman during the early years, Britt relied entirely on the daguerreotype process taught to him by Fitzgibbon. His equipment consisted of a small but heavy "quarter-plate box" of yellow oak, with bevelled ends and tight-fitting hinged doors. It had a precision Voigtlander lens, made in Vienna, to produce views on 3¼- by 4¼- inch, silver-coated copper plates.

In the year 1856, however, when Britt sold his pack train, he went to San Francisco and bought a "wholeplate" camera with a Petzval lens capable of producing 6½- by 8½-inch daguerreotype. He also learned to take the new photos known as ambrotypes, a glass negative with a black backing that gave the illusion of a positive print. Some of his images were even colored lightly.

Even the stern visage (below) of Jacksonville's minister reveals the skill with which Peter Britt overcame the limitations of his camera and the early photographic processes

The problem with both daguerreotypes and ambrotypes was that they were essentially one-of-a-kind pictures. There was no negative, and no good way existed to make extra copies. Nor did further record of them remain at Britt's gallery once he sold them. Thus there is little trace of his earliest work beyond the nearly 100 plates that survive to document Jacksonville's first decade of life.

A further complication with the early photographic processes was the need for painfully-long exposure times, with subjects often forced to sit in bright sunlight without moving for as much as 45 seconds. This fact alone accounted for the look of strained determination on the faces of many sitters.

To help keep customers motionless, Britt used complicated posing chairs and iron headclamps. The bases of these clamps are often seen in his full-length portraits as a third "foot." For his young customers Britt also employed a posing chair that had an arm hole at the back so that a parent could crouch out of sight and hold the child immobile.

But photographic developments came quickly in those years. Using the radically-new "wet-plate" process, Britt made his first paper photo in February, 1858. His subject was a rugged half-breed trapper posed in partial profile with a rifle on his shoulder.

A year later Britt introduced to southern Oregon the tintype, a photo made on black-enameled iron that was by far the cheapest and simplest of all picture processes.

The tintype gained acceptance in the Civil War years because it

Peter Britt,
Photographic Artist,
JACKSONVILLE, OREGON.

Ambrotypes,
Photographs,
Cartes de Visite

DONE IN THE FINEST STYLE OF ART.

Pictures Reduced
OR ENLARGED TO LIFE SIZE.

Early Britt newspaper advertisment (above) and Jacksonville's United States Hotel

stood the wear and tear of army mail and garrison life better than photos on paper, glass or polished silver.

By 1862, however, Britt was affected by the craze, started in Italy, for *cartes-de-visite*, small paper portraits gummed to the reverse side of calling cards. The little 2½- by 4-inch cartes transformed the photograph from a prized luxury secured only once or twice in a lifetime to a disposable item to be given to friends and purchased for less than three dollars a dozen.

The demand for cartes and the need to file them somewhere prompted the invention of what was later to become a family institution, the photograph album. More importantly, the carte established the supremacy of the collodion wet-plate process, since it alone could produce an infinite number of paper prints from one glass negative.

The introduction of the "cabinet photograph," a variety of larger paper print, posed a new test because flaws now became more conspicuous. But it also provided more latitude for experimentation, and some photographers began to concentrate on pose, lighting and sensitive treatment of facial characteristics.

If there was a particular Britt trademark, it was his talent for pose and composition — perhaps derived from his early training as a painter. A remarkably large number of his customers were captured in attitudes of graceful ease rather than stilted self-consciousness. Family portraits were particularly well done, with Britt perceptively having caught their sense of group solidarity.

Britt had a varied clientele. Jacksonville in the 1860's was not only the leading metropolis in Southern Oregon, but was also the recognized stopover for stagecoach traffic between California and points north. Britt took thousands of pictures of these wayfarers. The letters he received included many requests for additional prints and testify to his reputation as the best-known photographer in the Pacific Northwest.

In those days a significant part of Britt's business came from making portraits of the deceased. These were often coupled with pictures of the grieving widows beside freshly raised tombstones. Although this general practice was later abandoned as tasteless, many such negatives still survive in Britt's memorabilia.

Throughout the second half of the nineteenth century, no other variety of photograph could rival the popularity of the stereo view. The stereo card, with two nearly identical pictures mounted side-by-side, provided a stunning three-dimensional effect when viewed through an adjustable mechanism known as a stereoscope.

It provided, at a time before pictorial magazines or newspapers, a means to see life in foreign lands, the miracle of industrialization, the magnitude of disaster and the beauty of natural wonders. After the Civil War a home's parlor table was not complete without a stereoscope and a basket of views.

Sometime in the late 1860's Britt purchased his first double-barreled stereo camera and produced his own views. It was to be a watershed in his career, for it changed him from a sedentary gallery photographer to a roving chronicler of frontier scenes and landscapes.

Britt now became a full-fledged outdoor photographer, assembling a traveling outfit in a two-horse wagon with canvas cover. He christened his portable studio "The Pain," and it soon became a common sight in the mining settlements and mountains of southern Oregon and northern California.

Unlike most photographers, Britt refused to sell his stereo negatives to the few large companies with nationwide marketing facilities. Instead he fabricated his views in his studio, mounted many on orange cards and sold them for six dollars a dozen.

Because Britt sold his stereo cards almost exclusively to the walk-in trade, they are rare, with only some 60 examples extant. Moreover, many original negatives are gone, victims of misguided thrift in which the glass plates were scoured clean for reuse.

Despite his willingness to try each new studio process as it came along, it was in an outdoor photograph taken in 1874 that he achieved the great triumph of his career, the first picture ever taken of Crater Lake.

This 1,900-foot-deep lake lies in the crater of an extinct volcano among the Cascade Mountains, 87 miles northeast of Jacksonville. Known to the Klamath Indians as the "Dwelling Place of the Gods," Crater Lake was first discovered by prospectors in 1853 and periodically "rediscovered" over the next two decades. But it was never shown on any map until after Britt's photographs appeared.

Britt first accompanied an expedition to the lake in 1868 and again in 1869, but no photographs were secured. Finally, in 1874, Britt and his 12-year-old son Emil joined Captain O. C. Applegate and Samuel Hall in a new expedition to the rim.

They loaded Britt's wagon with camping gear and 200 pounds of photo equipment, including a standard wet plate camera, a stereo camera, a darkroom tent, 20 8- by 10-inch glass plates, assorted chemicals and a precious keg of distilled water.

The party spent five days traversing a distance that today's motorist can cover in two hours. Using a wagon road that passed just three miles from their destination, they then followed a trail blazed during the 1869 expedition. A final day of pulling and shoving brought the wagon to the brink of the crater, which rose vertically nearly 1,000 feet above the water of the lake.

The tricky wet-plate process required clear, sunny weather. For two days the men waited under stormy skies in the cold, windy discomfort of their meager camp. They drained the keg of water and melted snow from the few patches remaining in mid-August.

"The Pain," Peter Britt's photographic wagon

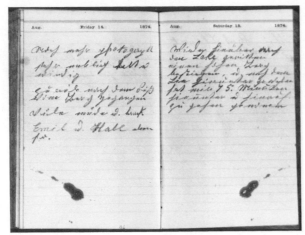
Entries in German from Peter Britt's diary on the days following his first photograph of Crater Lake

By the 1880's, Crater Lake had become a popular spot for visitors

On the third discouraging day they had just started to break camp in defeat when the fog and mist suddenly cleared. Britt quickly set up his black tent, coated several glass plates with liquid collodion and made two 20-second exposures from the campsite, looking northwards toward Wizard Island. Half an hour later, he emerged from the tent with two perfect negatives.

Britt's own diary entry for the epic occasion was typically brief and restrained:

> **Thursday, August 13, 1874**
> "Photographed the lake. Very cold and windy. Emil had a cough."

Although he made little of the achievement, it was remarkable. The photographs he took were probably the only ones ever made of Crater Lake by the "wet-plate process," and it was not until many years later that other photographers began to venture to the remote site.

Britt put Crater Lake on the map. Many people first saw that scenic landmark through the medium of Britt's stereograph views, which became so popular that they were pirated by other photographers and sold without credit or payment to Britt. The Crater Lake pictures served as models for lithographs used in commercial advertising, and the Portland Immigration Board featured half-tone reproductions of them in promotional pamphlets soon after the invention of photo-engraving.

A decade later William Gladstone Steel, a noted publisher and conservationist, began his campaign to save Crater Lake from private exploitation. He armed himself with Britt's pictures and journeyed to Washington. There he pitched himself into a long struggle that did not end until 1902, when an act of Congress created Crater Lake National Park and preserved 160,000 acres of breath-taking scenery. Britt's photographs probably were as critical a factor in Steel's effort as were those taken by William Henry Jackson in the fight to preserve Yellowstone as America's first national park.

Unlike Jackson, who covered thousands of miles to get his pictures of hot springs, waterfalls, geysers and sculptured canyons, Britt's photo wagon never strayed outside a 200-mile radius of Jacksonville. Contained within this small area were enough subjects to occupy Britt for several lifetimes.

He had the picturesque Pacific coastline, the nearly impenetrable redwood forests, the Rogue and Klamath river valleys, the Siskiyou Mountains and the deserts and lava beds east of the Cascades. In each of these settings, too, were pioneers as photogenic as Britt could have wished.

Britt's forays into the countryside proved a welcome relief from the same sort of problems as those that plague a modern commercial photographer, homely-looking customers who blame the camera operator when the likeness is not lovely to behold. To one such customer, a saloon-keeper's daughter, Britt once replied curtly: "Miss, if you want a beautiful face, you must bring one with you."

But the countryside rambles became even more frequent when Britt's wife Amalia succumbed to an intestinal disorder and died in 1871. Each summer thereafter Britt would pack his wagon, take his three children and venture into the countryside to record his impression of the vanishing frontier.

On these expeditions he became increasingly dissatisfied with the elaborate wet-plate process, its innumerable and breakable glass bottles, easily spilled chemicals, suffocating dark tent and clumsy developing and fixing trays. All this could be eliminated if a dry plate could be prepared at home, exposed in the field and developed after returning to the comforts of the studio.

Britt found his answer in the tannin dry plate, experimented with by amateurs but virtually ignored by professionals. The process required that a collodion plate be bathed in tannic acid, then dried in the dark. These plates could be carried for weeks without losing their sensitivity, although once they were exposed they had to be developed in 24 hours. This breakthrough was perfectly suited to Britt's short trips, and by 1877 he was taking most of his outdoor views with tannin dry plates.

The following year Emil, his teenaged son, began to work with his father in the studio. After he turned 20, Emil was apprenticed for a year in a San Francisco studio. In the meantime Britt enlarged his home again in anticipation of adding his son to the firm. Emil's training — he learned to use gelatin dry plates and to produce large 16- by 16-inch bust portraits — helped to keep the Britt gallery pre-eminent in Southern Oregon. Peter Britt meanwhile kept an active hand in all phases of the business until he retired at the age of 81.

A hand-painted tintype portrait

After a half-century career, Britt's achievements as a photographer were many and varied. Not the least was his ability to keep abreast of advances in the profession. He could duplicate new styles and processes within a year of their introduction, despite the vagaries of 19th century transportation and his out-of-the-way location.

In terms of quality, Britt's work compared with the best of the pioneer photographers and earned him the respect and praise of the many practitioners of his profession. In Washington, D.C., many who viewed his photographs considered him the equal of Civil War photographer Matthew Brady.

Britt had the technical proficiency to create striking portraits on porcelain. His large 11- by 14-inch tintypes are unique examples of excellence in an otherwise undistinguished genre. His

27

wet-plate prints of cloud-covered landscapes remain a puzzle to those who understand the limitations of the collodion process.

His lust for adventure, coupled with his technical excellence, had given birth to the Crater Lake pictures. He might have achieved much more had he been willing to wander still further from his gallery. As one example, the Modoc Indian War of 1872-73 was waged just 75 miles east of Jacksonville, but Britt ignored this unprecedented chance to document the last of California's Indian Wars.

Nevertheless, such wandering probably would have marred his prime benefit to history, for out of his sedentary life in Jacksonville came his matchless pictorial record of 50 years in the life of a single western community.

While his half-century duration in Jacksonville may well mark Britt's chief value as a photographer today, to his contemporaries the man from Switzerland with the brown hair, bushy beard and oval face displayed a multitude of talents and indulged himself in a bewildering array of commerical ventures.

The earliest of Britt's outside interests had been his fleeting entanglement as a gold miner and the operation of a mule-train packing business which provided him with his first financial success. But his most notable and consuming passion was his gardens, which became the cradle of horticulture in Southern Oregon.

Britt had an obsessive desire to demonstrate that Oregon's Rogue River Valley was a semi-tropical paradise. Joining him in his wish were land promoters and newspaper editors who, in their zeal, misleadingly labeled their region "the Italy of the Pacific" and "the Eden of Oregon." They persisted in describing the climate as "Mediterranean" when in fact the region is better known for its hot, rainless summers frequently followed by three seasons of cool, wet weather.

Britt buttressed these claims with his endless experiments. These started in 1857 when he purchased an entire load of fruit and grape cuttings from an Italian peddler who had traveled along the Siskiyou trail from California. The cuttings included a "snow apple," a "pound pear," and a peach tree. Each of these three was considered to have been the first of its type in Southern Oregon, and each lived into the 20th century — the apple was finally destroyed by fire and the peach in a heavy snowfall.

At the same time, Britt received a copy of *The American Fruit Culturist,* which served both as horticultural text and English language grammar for the German-speaking immigrant. Subsequently Britt developed a 20-acre orchard on his ranch one mile north of Jacksonville, where he experimented with Bartlett pears and pioneered the use of smudgepots to protect the trees from late frosts. His was the first orchard in the Rogue Valley, and by 1860

Even though Peter Britt's career as a miner was brief, others continued prospecting for gold until late in the century

28

Britt was selling peaches, apples, and pears to his neighbors. Today he is honored as the father of the region's multi-million dollar fruit industry.

The orchard was but a small part of Britt's estate. He had 80 acres called "The Forest" behind his house, and the five acres immediately surrounding the residence came to be known as Britt Park. Here, dry hillside was transformed into a terraced, landscaped garden with fieldstone retaining walls. Excavating was done by shovel and wheelbarrow, and he constructed a mile-long irrigation ditch and installed an elaborate system of underground irrigation pipes from the headwaters of Jackson Creek to the undulating slopes of his park — at a time when other settlers were watering their gardens by hand. In time, most of the flowers, ornamental shrubs and non-indigenous trees of the area's early settlers came from Britt Park.

Structures that were scattered through the grounds included a combination barn and granary, a water tower, carriage house, root cellar, and winery. There also was a masonry fountain and a stone lilypond stocked with goldfish.

To landscape the park Britt acquired plants from most of the civilized world, importing many across the country from a Philadelphia nursery. He brought in huge rhododendrons, sweet bay trees and an immense Chinese wisteria with drooping clusters of purple flowers. German edging which still grows on Jacksonville's walkways had its start in Britt Park, as did the ivy which still clings to many of the town's buildings. Britt procured the ivy from a British firm at the skyhigh price of five dollars a set.

Typical of Britt's nearly manic effort to prove that the valley was a part of the tropics was the palm tree that grew in the front yard, the first and largest of that variety in Oregon. Britt planted the seed just before he embarked on his epic picture making expedition to Crater Lake. On his return, he found that a sprout had pushed through the earth. Each autumn thereafter he built a little house over the tree to protect it, a job that required scaffolding when the tree approached a height of 30 feet. Also growing in the yard was the equally exotic and troublesome Abyssinian banana, the same species that was often represented in ancient Egyptian sculpture. Each fall the giant plant had to be removed from the ground and placed indoors for the winter.

The Britt solarium housed cactus, kumquats, pomegranates, lemons, oranges and coffee trees. They all bloomed and bore fruit. In the park was further "proof" of the region's "mild and favored clime" — two 60-foot Monterey cypress, a magnolia, a fragrant olive, some sort of inedible wild orange and two Japanese persimmon trees. His greatest success came with the cultivation of Smyrna figs from carefully propagated trees.

A stray nut which accidentally fell into an expensive, imported

The gothic Britt home amid the lush vegetation of Britt Park

shipment of other items even grew into a wide-spreading English chestnut tree that for half a century never failed to bear an abundant crop of nuts. In fact, the only recorded failure of a Britt import was a eucalyptus brought in as a seed from Australia which died in cold weather, a fatality duly noted by the Jacksonville *Reveille* newspaper.

Britt Park became the showplace of southern Oregon. For 20 years it was featured in most northwest railroad advertising. All early Chamber of Commerce literature had pictures of the Britt home and its banana, palm and gingko trees. It was only after the family was gone that the garden became overgrown and its tropical imports perished.

Britt's green thumb also extended to vineyards. He had noticed the luxuriant grapes that grew wild in the valley and concluded that domestic varieties could also thrive. He secured cuttings from the mission grapevines of California and, family tradition has it, by 1858 Britt was making the first wine in the Territory.

He eventually experimented with more than 200 varieties of grapes, ranging for advice as far as the German Wine Growers' Association on the Rhine. He built a sophisticated press house and imported two 1,000-gallon redwood fermenting tanks.

By 1880 his 15-acre vineyard was producing up to 3,000 gallons a year. Records show that he made a very popular claret, along with muscatel, schiller, zinfandel and port. He charged 50 cents a gallon, plus the cost of cask and freight, and one of his first customers was the local Roman Catholic priest, Father Blanchet. It was his endorsement that provided Britt the custom of much of the Oregon Diocese. Other regular clients were the stagecoach lines and saloons. Largely through Britt's efforts viticulture had become a significant industry in the Rogue Valley by 1890.

Another product, marketed under Britt's label and distributed throughout Southern Oregon, was honey, an outgrowth of Britt's experiments with bees to get better pollination for his orchards and vineyards. The apiary eventually grew into a profitable enterprise of its own, with general stores throughout the valley stocking jars of honey from the 35 Britt hives.

One Britt enterprise, done purely as a public service and not for financial gain, was his daily log of weather conditions. Britt steadfastly maintained these logs and his family continued them after he died, a weather diary of nearly 100 years. Like his pictorial record of Jacksonville, Britt's climactic chronicle bequeathed a wealth of knowledge about the Rogue River Valley's weather through the years.

The entries recorded daily observations on temperature, precipitation, wind velocity, cloud cover, crop conditions, and forest fire danger. Britt began it in the 1850's before there was a government weather agency. He used only a pocket sun dial and a home-

First wine for the region came from carefully tended Britt vineyards

30

made rain gauge, originally writing his notes in German script. His early reports refer to dried-up wells, the migration of swallows, the croaking of frogs before each storm and his concern for the effects of weather on the spread of contagious disease.

When Congress set up a weather service within the Army Signal Corps in 1870, it enlisted volunteer civilian observers. Britt was designated the official reporter for Jacksonville, and was provided with thermometers and a rain gauge. While he contributed regular reports and occasionally even wrote sober articles for the Signal Corps' monthly journal, Britt could also note with wry humor that the readings of one day's record in 1889 were ruined by a boy who broke the rain gauge with his slingshot.

Britt, who first arrived in Southern Oregon with five dollars in his pocket, had financed his fledgling studio through the high-risk ventures of mining and mule-packing. A later and more profitable pursuit was his practice of moneylending. In this he filled a void left by Jacksonville's bank, which allegedly never made a loan in its history.

The interest usually charged was 10 per cent, though in one instance a rate of 60 per cent was established. Acreage was the usual security, but one chattel mortgage offered a "bay mule named Jenney and one black mule mare named Mag."

An unusual aspect of these financial affairs was Britt's favored relationship with the Chinese community which, in 1874, numbered more than 600 in Jackson County. Most merchants treated the "Celestials" with contempt and refused their business. The local press made frequent racial slurs and lobbied for a "head tax" on Orientals.

In all of Jacksonville only Britt and one other man, a lawyer named Wesley Kahler, seemed to have any sympathy for these pariahs. For his part, Britt allowed a Chinese company to mine on his property in the 1850's in return for a portion of the profits. He gave grubstakes to Chinese miners in the following decades when they took over abandoned gold claims. He became a landlord to several Chinese families, keeping a special rentbook for their signatures, and permitted Chinese to live in several shanties on his own property.

Britt also acquired a large amount of choice real estate, first through foreclosures as a result of his moneylending, but later as a conscious investment based on his belief in the Rogue River Valley's future. By the turn of the century Britt owned more land in Southern Oregon than any other individual.

When the Oregon and California Railroad was completed through the Rogue Valley, it brought with it a long-sought access to the markets of Portland and San Francisco. This, in turn, sparked a real estate boom. In the late 1880's, Easterners poured in, many of them intent on becoming "orchard gentry." With

Chinese miner

deeds to more than 2,000 acres of tillable land, Britt was in a favorable position to add to his fortune.

As his prosperity increased so did his civic stature. A responsible elder of the town, Britt remained on friendly terms with all the local clergymen yet was a confirmed skeptic on religious matters. He was an ardent follower of Robert Ingersoll, the Great Agnostic, and once served as vice-president of the Oregon State Secular Union.

Instead of religion he was drawn to the social groupings and fraternal orders of the large German-Swiss minority that played a major role in determining the tenor and scope of life in the mining settlements. The four major ethnic organizations were the Turnverein, Eintracht, Harmonie and Stamm — and, to varying degrees, the Britt family was active in all four. As members, Britt and others could preserve and celebrate their Swiss origins while contributing to the community good works and cultural enrichment.

Jacksonville's Silver Cornet Band

To the casual observer, Jacksonville in its early days was a wide-open mining town high in the Siskiyou Mountains, miles from the nearest railroads and markets and culturally isolated. But it became the musical center of the Pacific coast, in large measure because of its German-speaking citizens and their penchant for choral and instrumental music.

Almost as soon as the town was founded there sprang up the Jacksonville Harmonie, a loose musical association which sponsored a string band, German singing club, silver cornet band, individual instruction in music, and a brass band.

Elsewhere when musicians attempted to play a Hadyn symphony they were pelted with eggs and vegetables by crowds baying for *Yankee Doodle.* Fiddler's contests, jigs, and folk tunes were virtually the only acceptable musical events, and most Oregon audiences were more receptive to minstrels than Mozart.

But in Jacksonville almost everyone in the population of 1,500 had a musical instrument, despite the fact that getting one was no easy matter. For his 12-year-old daughter, Britt bought a new Steinway which cost $700 and weighed over 1,000 pounds. The piano was shipped by boat from San Francisco to Portland, transferred to a boxcar for a rail trip to Roseburg, and then hauled the last 100 miles to Jacksonville by buckboard.

A survey once found a total of five spinets in Jacksonville dating from this period — as many at the time as there were in the entire state of California.

Britt was a loyal patron of the musical arts, sang with the German Singing Club, gave over his grounds for recitals, and provided lessons for his children.

He was also a zealous convert to the lodges and secret societies that then were the rage. The non-Catholic Germans and Swiss waxed most enthusiastic about *The Improved Order of Red*

Men which, despite its name, was a whites-only organization. Its aims beyond that of a full and often raucous social life were never clearly stated, but for many it seemed a comfortable substitute for the traditional religious forms.

The vigor of the German-Swiss community extended into politics as well, and for many years the German vote was a dominant force in Southern Oregon. Britt was not immune, and he was elected twice to the Jacksonville Town Council — although he seemed to have preferred to serve the community through its various volunteer and appointive committees.

Jacksonville became sharply divided over the issues raised by the Civil War. Many citizens had come from border states and were fiercely pro-Confederate. The German-speaking community, however, remained loyal to the Union. Britt, who came to manhood in a weakened and divided Swiss Confederation which had reverted to near-feudalism, contributed heavily to the Union Sanitary Fund.

Later, Britt and most of his ethnic kin drifted from a liberal to a more conservative stance, through the cumulative effects of time, prosperity, and Americanization. At one time a Democrat, Britt became convinced the currency policies of the Silver Democrats were irresponsible. He permanently transferred his allegiance to the Republicans in the 1880's.

Britt had seen to it that his children were thoroughly assimilated and Americanized. But in his declining years his thoughts drifted more to his native Europe and to his earliest training there, as an artist. He turned again to his easel and palette and spent many hours in his skylit studio painting from memory that landscapes of Mount Blanc, Lake Geneva and views of his beloved Switzerland. He also did portraits of his family and renditions of the scene of his greatest photographic triumph, Crater Lake.

He spent hours on his balcony surveying the Rogue River Valley through a telescope or taking solitary walks in the cool evening. The years in which he had neared and reached retirement had coincided with Jacksonville's decline in importance. Many friends and leading citizens had moved to Medford, Portland or even San Francisco before the turn of the century.

Peter Britt as an elderly man amid his garden (top), and a scene he painted from his greatest triumph, Crater Lake's first photograph

Despite his advanced age he traveled to see his friends often. He wrote more frequently to his kinsmen in Switzerland and even thought of returning there. A further testament of his loneliness and cultural isolation was his voracious reading of German language periodicals as he sat in his solarium among his exotic plants.

In 1905, Jackson County was to have an exhibit at an exposition in Portland. On display would be many of the products and resources of Southern Oregon — fruit, wines, minerals, photographs and literature about the remarkable Mediterranean climate.

33

In Loving Remembrance of

Peter Britt

DIED OCTOBER 3 1905   AGED 87 YEARS

Probably no other man had devoted so much of his life to promoting these things. Britt's son Emil had been appointed to the committee responsible for the exhibit — and Peter, though now 86, insisted on going to Portland alone to see that Southern Oregon received proper recognition.

He spent a week in September, at the fair drum-beating the virtues of his adopted region, as he had done all his life. Returning by train, he contracted a cold which developed into pneumonia. The aged photographer lingered for a week, then died on October 3, 1905, at the Jacksonville residence in which he had lived for 53 years.

Today, thousands of his photographic images rest in the Southern Oregon Historical Society's Jacksonville Museum. Captured in silver and brown on the Daguerreotypes, ambrotypes and glass plate negatives is a wealth of knowledge about the growth of one small town, from its start as a booming, 1850's mining camp to its maturity as a prosperous commercial center. Represented in the collection are graphic examples of every aspect of life on the Oregon frontier — a monument to Peter Britt's inner vision.

Peter Britt was a solid representative of the pioneer cameramen who invaded the settler's west. His life and his impact on early photography remain keys to the rich heritage of the Pacific Northwest.

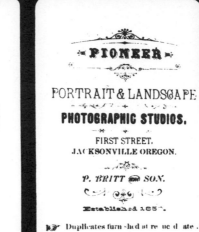

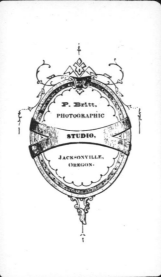

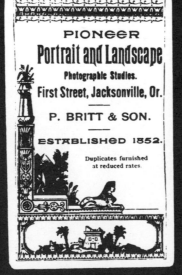

Notes About the Plates

by Peter E. Palmquist

Peter Britt's significance to photography lies as much in his craft as in his art. His unique images of the frontier's people, scenery and events owe equally to his mastery of the fledgling techniques of photography and his artistic talents.

Originally a portrait painter, Britt carried into photography the essential abilities needed to produce fine art — composition, design, color sense and the like. Moreover, he was a man absorbed with the intricacy of how things work.

Even as a portrait painter, Britt had learned — out of necessity — to grind minerals and herbs to make pigments, mix his own oils, tie brushes and weave canvas. In his other interests, Britt had displayed keen awareness of the mechanics and techniques of, for example, bee-keeping, horticulture, weather observation and house construction.

It should be borne in mind that Britt plunged into photography less than a decade after Louis Daguerre announced in January, 1839, the process which bears his name. The field was fresh, the techniques ever-changing. It was hard to keep abreast of new advances, especially for a German-speaking immigrant working away from the beaten track.

When Britt decided to join the swelling ranks of daguerreotype practitioners, he was astute enough to apprentice himself to J. H. Fitzgibbon of St. Louis. Other photographers had merely learned the infant art's rudiments before trundling westward with the cumbersome equipment that marked their trade in search of customers for "portraits drawn by Helios, god of the sun."

Britt stayed in St. Louis with Fitzgibbon, a recognized leader in his field and a man with a flair for self-promotion. When the daguerreotype process was popularly announced to America through the 1839 writings of Lewis Clark, Fitzgibbon was electrified by the news. By 1841 he was a practicing daguerrean. Six years later, his abilities behind the camera and his skills at publicity had drawn national attention to his gallery.

Public reaction to the products of daguerrean artists like Fitzgibbon and Britt was immediate. Comments in newspapers of the time about the daguerrotype included such remarks as, "Their exquisite perfection almost transcends the bounds of sober

Peter Britt

(page opposite) A few of the many logographs used by Peter Britt to identify his paper prints and tintypes

belief . . .'' "There is not an object, even the most minute, embraced in that wide scope (of the daguerreotype) which was not in the original; and it is impossible that one should have been omitted. Think of that!"

Now, more than 120 years later, an observer would not be so incredulous. But these mirror-surfaced images, even today, retain a quality that sets them apart from other photographic artifacts. The viewer, opening the hinged case of a daguerreotype, beholds a dazzling mirror of light. Upon closer inspection, a silvery film appears to cloud the reflective surface. When the case is slowly rotated to change the viewing angle, the image suddenly reaches its full grandeur. Every minute detail of a century-old scene comes into sharp relief. One famous French painter of Daguerre's day, seeing his first daguerreotype, commented, "From today, painting is dead!"

The process by which light was fixed into a permanent image on the silver surface of the daguerreotype was an incredible accomplishment. The result of nearly 13 years' work by Daguerre and a fellow Frenchman, Joseph Niepce, the daguerreotype relied on chemical reactions between light, silver, iodine and mercury.

A copper sheet was first plated with a thin layer of silver, then buffed and cleaned until it was without blemish. The prepared silver surface was exposed to fumes of iodine in an airtight box, which turned it a delicate golden yellow in five to thirty minutes. During that time reactions between the metallic silver and the iodine formed a light sensitive compound, silver iodide, and the plate became ready for use.

After exposure in the camera the plate was developed even though it still bore no visible trace of the image. By supporting the exposed plate in a closed box filled with fumes of heated mercury, a chemical reaction would begin to take place in the areas which had been touched by light. After a few minutes an image, composed of an amalgam of mercury and silver, became visible. Even more reflective than the silver upon which it rested, the amalgam highlights of the daguerreotype were revealed in a dazzling, mirror-like brightness, while the deep, black tones of the shadow areas were made up of the original silver plate. Viewed from the proper angle, these shadows reflected almost no light.

Because the developed daguerreotype remained sensitive to light until every trace of unexposed silver iodide was removed, the first experimental images obtained by Daguerre quickly tarnished and clouded into obscurity. Bathing the developed plate in a strong solution of common salt provided one method of removing the unexposed silver iodide and "fixed" the image. But it was the discovery of hyposulfite of soda, an easily obtained, quick to use fixing agent, which made the daguerreotype commercially successful. After fixing the plate in this solution, which rapidly became the familiar "hypo" of the photographer's darkroom, the plate was washed, dried and mounted under glass to protect its delicate surface.

Except for minor alterations and improvements to increase the sensitivity and permanence of the plate, the daguerreotype process described was the same one used by Fitzgibbon when he first met Britt.

Britt quickly learned to produce daguerreotypes but stayed with Fitzgibbon until he also had acquired a unique understanding of the photographers' trade. When Britt left St. Louis to return to Highland in 1848, he was already better prepared for success than hundreds of his fellow artists.

Peter Britt's Highland daguerreotypes captured the spirit of the citizens of that small town. Today, only a half-dozen images are known to exist from his first studio, but even these few samples display his consummate knowledge of daguerrean techniques.

To fully appreciate young Britt's efforts, it should be remembered that posing for a daguerreotype was a procedure totally unlike that experienced in a modern photographic studio. After the plate was sensitized, the subject sat — or sometimes stood — in a rigid position during the exposure. To insure rigidity, iron head braces, special posing chairs and other "torture-chamber" paraphernalia were employed. Additionally, the prolonged exposure time required absolutely fixed facial expressions to avoid movement. This explains why many of our ancestors, viewed in early photographs, appear to be rigid, upright puritans and sour-faced, starched pioneers.

Despite the difficulties that early techniques and processes imposed, Britt's first Highland daguerreotypes represented a great accomplishment. His subjects, unlike those of less skillful artists, retained their natural expressions and appeared, for the most part, comfortable. It was a skill that Britt carried west in 1852, when he left Illinois and journeyed overland to Oregon.

For at least the first seven years following his arrival in Jacksonville, Britt utilized the daguerreotype process. His quarter-plate (3¼- by 4¼-inch) camera was purchased under the direction of Fitzgibbon and represented a quality instrument which was to serve him well on the frontier. Most of the earliest surviving Britt photographs were taken with this camera.

The subsequent purchase of a full-plate (6½- by 8½-inch) camera allowed him to prepare a full range of the most popular sized images for his clients. Surviving examples include sixth-plate (2¾- by 3¼-inches), quarter-plate, half-plate (4¼- by 6½-inches) and at least one full-plate. Britt did not commonly sign or label his earliest works, and attribution of these images to him has been made through various recognized studio props as well as stylistic considerations.

Posing stand

Peter Britt's quarter plate (3¼- by 4¼-inch) daguerreotype camera, lens cap for making exposures, daguerreotype in open case, with closed daguerreotype case, and unused daguerreotype plates with original plate box

(top) Sixth plate (2¾- by 3¼-inch) daguerreotype showing mirror writing, (middle) sixth plate daguerreotype of Peter Britt in case with brass mat and preserver, and velvet cover lining, and (bottom) sixth plate daguerreotype case with mother of pearl inlay on black lacquer with gilt design

(page opposite) Posing in the Britt Studio before a painted backdrop

Because of the lack of a negative step in the daguerreotype process the image produced was usually reversed left-to-right, a fact that made many wedding rings appear to be on the right hand. While this was not usually a problem in portraiture, it was undesirable in outdoor scenes that included shop signs or well-known topography. But all of Britt's daguerreotype views of Jacksonville are "right-reading." Whether he re-photographed the original plate or used a mirror is not definitely known, but use of a mirror seems most likely.

Peter Britt's first daguerreotype camera still exists and is at the Jacksonville Museum in Jacksonville, Oregon, the major repository of Britt artifacts. Built by Voigtlander and Sohn of Vienna, this camera and other artifacts from Britt's early studio provides insight into his photographic methods.

Also present in the museum collection are many samples of miniature daguerreotype cases, constructed of wood covered with leather or papier mache, or made entirely of thermoplastic materials. The latter heat-formed plastic cases date as early as 1853 and represent the first large-scale commercial use of plastic substances. Many of the items in the collection are beautiful to examine, are decorated with raised cover embossures, brass fittings and handsome velvet linings. They are ideal complements to Britt's early images.

Unfortunately no easy method existed, during this early period of photography, to produce multiple copies of an image other than by additional sittings or through laborious copying of the original. An early paper-negative process known as the calotype or talbotype originated in England at about the same time as the daguerreotype. It failed to become popular in the West, however, because of restrictive patent requirements and the process's inability to render fine detail.

In 1851, Frederick Archer announced the greatest breakthrough to occur in the craft of photography since Daguerre's efforts of more than a decade before. Known as collodion, his discovery provided an easily-usable method of binding light-sensitive emulsions to a glass base. Collodion was a viscous solution of nitrated-cotton dissolved in ether. This liquid was poured onto the middle of the plate while the photographer held the glass by its edges and tilted it back and forth, until the glass was evenly coated. Collodion was not light sensitive itself, but it held the light-sensitive silver salt firmly in suspension while the picture was taken and developed. In many different forms, Archer's discovery became known as the wet-plate process.

By the mid-1850's, a version of the wet-plate process — known as the ambrotype — had achieved great popularity. Much cheaper and more light sensitive than the clumsy daguerreotypes, the ambrotype replaced its predecessor's metal support with a glass

plate. After coating the glass with collodion, the plate was sensitized by bathing it in a silver nitrate solution. It was then exposed in the camera while still damp and developed immediately, since it lost sensitivity as it dried.

To create an ambrotype, the artist placed the finished wet-plate negative emulsion side up and backed it with a black surface of asphaltum, varnish, japanned iron or velvet. It was mounted in a miniature case in the same manner as the daguerreotypes. When viewed by reflected light, the negative appeared as a positive. Less expensive and without the glare of the mirror-like daguerreotype, ambrotypes soon became popular, though still a one-of-a-kind photographs.

Most remarkable among many of Britt's ambrotypes is one of Jacksonville under a disastrous winter's flood. Taken under marginal light conditions, this view ranks among the first photojournalistic efforts in the West.

Even while Britt continued to use daguerreotypes and ambrotypes, his interest extended to new technical advances. One of these, the melainotype (an early name for the ferrotype or tintype) utilized the application of the collodion emulsion directly onto a surface of japanned tin. These plates, identified by "Forneff melainotype, pat. 1856," are well represented in the Britt holdings at the Jacksonville Museum. Especially fine is one circa 1858, which has as its subject probably the first black woman in the Oregon Territory.

Still another variation of the collodion emulsion was its application directly on leather. Several of Britt's leathertypes exist today, as do images on opal glass and ambrotypes made on ruby-colored glass which eliminated the need for backing the plate.

The first commercial production of photographs on paper using the wet-collodion process occurred circa 1852. Britt made his first paper print on February 10, 1858, one of the earliest in the West to do so. Unlike most of its predecessors, a paper print was truly inexpensive and multiple copies could be produced at will.

Among his early experiments with paper prints, Britt attempted to introduce color into his photographs through an uncommon method, known as the hellenotype. Basically a pair of paper prints, the image was made up of two parts. One image was printed very faintly, then rendered transparent through the application of varnish. After the varnish had dried, the back of this light, translucent print was tinted with color to imitate the original scene. A darker print of the same image provided the second half. When the varnished print was registered over the darker image, the picture appeared to be in color.

Sometime before 1862, the growing craze for *cartes de visite*, calling cards with small photographs attached, extended west to

Quarter Plate ambrotype (see text) with many abrasions from misuse

Britt's studio. Special cameras with four or more lenses frequently were used and enabled a subject to have many photographs taken simultaneously. These paper prints were affixed to sturdy cards, usually 2½- by 4-inches in size. Thousands were sent through the mails, given to friends and used for business.

Like all of the other photographic processes that Peter Britt had mastered, the paper print required grueling hours of preparation. The printing paper itself originally was prepared by sizing the paper with a salt and albumen coating taken from the white of an egg. As photographers began to obtain their supplies ready-made from manufacturers, enormous quantities of eggs were required to fill their orders — the largest printing paper manufacturer in Europe reported he had used over 18,000,000 eggs per year.

Before use, the paper was sensitized by floating it in a tray containing silver nitrate solution, then dried. Since the sensitivity rapidly declined, new paper was prepared for each day's use. The final photograph was made by placing the paper in contact with the negative in a printing frame and then exposing the frame to direct sunlight. On overcast days, printing on the insensitive albumen paper sometimes took hours. Produced in great volume, these likeness include society figures, tradesmen, ruffians, nuns, babies, soldiers and animals.

In 1867 Britt introduced a larger version of the paper print, known as the cabinet photograph. The 4- by 7-inch images provided increased clarity of detail and stimulated more elaborate studio settings. Thousands of cartes de visite and cabinet photographs exist in the Jacksonville Museum, and they provide a unique glimpse into the changing styles and customs of Jacksonville. Britt's studio props and many trends in posing styles during the 1860's and 1870's are also clearly revealed. This is nowhere more clearly visible than in Britt's tintypes of the period.

The ubiquitous tintype, a distinctly American form of photography, proliferated as a companion to the cartes de visite. Produced on thin, black iron plates, the tintype captured the fancy of America because of its cheapness and durability. A substantial number of Britt tintypes exist. They are displayed alone, in carte de visite sized mounts, in frames and in photographic albums. They range in size from tiny (¾- by 1-inch) to the large (11- by14-inches). These last are unusually large and again indicate Britt's facility with the technical side of photography.

The unique popularity of the tintype lasted until the last years of the century. By the 1870's, vignetted head and shoulder portraits began replacing the full-figure poses typical of the 1860's. His methods of posing reflected the improvements that burgeoning technology had brought to the trade. The wet-plate collodion process, while still woefully slow by modern standards, was a substantial improvement over the earliest processes. Expo-

Carte de Visite **of Jacob Grob, Peter Britt's stepson, with a Becker's stereoscope viewer, part of Britt's studio equipment**

sures were now measured in seconds rather than minutes, and subjects were able to pose in a more lifelike manner.

It was about this time, in the early 1870's, that Britt began adding decorative backgrounds as studio props. Many of these he painted himself, while the remainder were drawn from photographic supply houses. Amid forest scenes, stairways, colonnades and porticos, Jacksonville's residents began appearing in costumed poses befitting the town's advance into respectability.

It was also at this time that Britt turned more and more to outdoor photography, training his camera on the scenic beauty of southern Oregon and achieving his greatest successes as a pictorialist.

Contemporary with the views of Yellowstone by William Henry Jackson and the images of Yosemite by Edweard Muybridge and Carlton Watkins, Britt's photographs of the region stand both the test of time and the challenges of professional scrutiny.

As technical masterpieces, these photographs are remarkable. His first photograph of Crater Lake, for instance, was taken by the wet-plate process. Britt's pictures of this subject stand unique. The wet-plate collodion process is very sensitive to the color blue, and white clouds in a blue sky photograph without exception as a uniform shade of gray. In Britt's Crater Lake scenes, however, the cloud-filled sky is clearly visible — a technical accomplishment in mute contradiction to the limits of the chemical processes he used.

Amid his other outdoor photographs, a small number of "orange mount" stereographs also exist from this period. In preparing a stereograph, a pair of pictures was taken. When viewed through the means of a hand-held or parlor stereo viewer, they provided a startling illusion of depth that duplicated the original scene. Few of Britt's stereographs exist today, however, since he marketed them himself rather than through national firms, and most copies were lost. Perhaps 60 still exist in Jacksonville.

A few years later, Britt used the tannin dry plate to extend his efforts. In this process the usual wet-plate was sensitized and then bathed in a solution of alcohol and tannic acid, which allowed plates to be stored for a number of days or weeks before they lost their usefulness. This was ideal for Britt's brief excursions, allowing him to photograph outdoors without carrying a dark-tent. The tannin dry plate was not widely used by professional photographers, and once again Britt stands unique in his success with this medium.

In 1883, Emil Britt officially joined his father's business. Having spent the previous year at the famous firm of Bradley and Rulofson in San Francisco, Emil brought the gelatin dry-plate to the Britt operation. Although various dry plate methods had been used in the past, it was the introduction of the gelatin dry-plate in

Emil Britt at Crater Lake, August, 1874

(page opposite) Peter Britt's wagon and dark tent, used while making outdoor scenes by the wet-plate process, shown here at Crater Lake

45

1881 which provided a thoroughly reliable product. If any disadvantage existed with the new plates, it was the inability to re-use them when the image proved unsatisfactory. Most photographers of the frontier west found this problem minor by comparison to their advantage over wet-plates, however.

Emil's participation freed Peter to apply his painting skills to photography. He prepared many oversized photographic portraits which were embellished through the use of pastels, india ink and oil paints. Today many of these large portraits grace the walls of the Jacksonville Museum and reflect Britt's painterly training. A number of large tintypes were also hand-painted before being placed in the elaborate frames characteristic of the period. Intended to dominate the Victorian parlor, these family likenesses were highly prized by Britt's wealthier clientele. He also enjoyed photographing and coloring still lifes.

Attribution of the thousands of original negatives which date from Emil and Peter's partnership has been very difficult, although some distinction may be made on the basis of the camera format used. Nearly 8,000 negatives exist in the collection. Some 15 different format sizes are represented, ranging from 3¼- by 4¼- inches to 18- by 22-inches. As in many similar collections of photographic memorabilia, there are some negatives which appear to be the work of other photographers. These, together with additional thousands of original Britt images, form an incredible legacy of more than half a century of photographic technique. To study the Britt photographic artifacts is to study almost the entire spectrum of Nineteenth Century photography.

In preparing the original daguerreotypes, ambrotypes, melainotypes, leathertypes, opalotypes, cyanotypes, tintypes, wet- and dry-plate negatives and paper prints for reproduction in this volume, it was nearly impossible to choose the 70 best examples of Britt's work. To date, no attempt has been made to fully catalogue the material attributed to Peter Britt. Such a task would be monumental, since the Britt collection includes memorabilia on almost every aspect of early frontier photography.

More than four-fifths of Britt's entire output were portraits. The remainder comprise an astonishing array of his pictorial efforts. In making the final selections for this volume, the editors' choice was restricted to representative examples rather than proportional ones. Therefore, as in all portfolios which are not also *catalogues raisonne*, the inclusion of a particular image may place undue stress on a single aspect of Peter Britt's lengthy career.

The Britt collection in Jacksonville is a legacy not only to the State of Oregon but to the people of America. Peter Britt's importance as a regional photographer is paralleled by the remarkable insight that his work gives to the period of western expansion and the origins of photography.

A portion of the camera and studio equipment preserved in the Peter Britt Collection at the Jacksonville Museum

(page opposite) Peter Britt (1819-1905)

Portfolio

Peter Britt's daguerreotype of Joseph Suppiger's daughters, taken in Highland, Illinois in 1847, was typical of the fledgling photographer's first portraits. During the four years that Britt operated his Highland studio, he photographed many leading citizens and their families. Today, only a handful of these images have survived.

Among the most interesting of Britt's Highland daguerreotypes was this photograph taken of Prince Paul of Wurttemberg. His highness visited America during November, 1849 while engaged in a royal hunting safari for bison, antelope, bear and elk. The prince was also a well-respected painter. He posed for Peter Britt's camera attired in an artist's smock and holding one of his canvases.

52

The rugged boom town of Table Rock City which later became Jacksonville was a far cry from civilized Highland, Illinois. Yet, even in its earliest years, it must have held promise for young Britt, for he passed by the Willamette and Columbia river town of Portland to settle in the Siskiyou Mountains of southern Oregon.

With seven or more months on the trail separating them from loved ones left behind, Jacksonville residents took great pleasure in letters from home. Britt realized that "where so much gold was being found, I could undoubtedly do well in my business," and became prosperous by providing the miners with photographs.

The frontier years of Jacksonville were brief. By about 1860, when this ambrotype was taken, it had changed from a boom town to the dominant community in a growing agricultural region. The Eagle Hotel in nearby Ashland was a stagecoach stop for travelers entering Oregon from California.

Early in the 1860's, Jacksonville was stricken by a disasterous flood, which covered the town. Peter Britt photographed the calamity despite the cloudy, dim light and pouring rain. In his view, two men can be seen hip-deep in water, struggling to break a debris dam which diverted the flowing stream across nearby fields and into the town.

Even while Britt was still using daguerreotypes and ambrotypes to create his studio portraits, he learned of the newly-invented wet-plate collodion negative process. His first successful paper print, made on February 10, 1858, was of a half-breed trapper. The new technique quickly became a mainstay of the Britt photographic studio. Unmatched by either of the earlier methods, it required much shorter exposure times and could easily produce multiple prints of successful poses.

As Jacksonville increased in respectability, it attracted growing numbers of women. Included were a handful of blacks. When the state constitution's Free Negro Admission Article of 1857 was rejected, however, all of these were forced to leave. Only the Union victory that ended the Civil War concluded the apartheid policies of the region.

Non-Catholic German and Swiss residents of the town became zealous converts to the American craze for lodges and secret societies. While many were content to join the Masons and Odd Fellows, scores of others became enthusiastic converts to lesser known organizations, such as the whites-only Improved Order of Red Men Lodge.

Peter Britt's first portraits of Jacksonville's citizens had revealed frontiersmen and ladies clad in rough clothes against stark backgrounds. As the town matured, crinoline gowns replaced homespun, and plain walls gave way to ornate backdrops of Grecian columns and landscaped fields.

With the advent of the *cartes de visite*, small photographs fastened by adhesive to calling cards, many prominent members of town society posed before the Britt camera. The tiny *cartes* were popular, and thousands were exchanged by mail or traded between friends. Today, many of Britt's portraits in this medium exist only as inclusions in family photographic albums and are scattered throughout the country.

The *cartes de visite* also opened Britt's studio to other levels of society. As the price of a portrait sitting drew within the reach of the common townspeople and was no longer a once in a lifetime experience, thousands of pictures were taken of people from all walks of life.

Oftentimes, Peter Britt posed his
subjects simply. While many of
his competitors throughout the
United States followed stereo-
typed formulas in placing their
customers, Britt's painterly
training was reflected in his
photographs. The position of a
hand, a subject's gaze, the addition of a flower or the sugges-
tion of a gesture often made a
photograph memorable.

63

Jacksonville, by the close of the 1860's, had grown from a rough-hewn camp of log cabins and tents to a burgeoning community in which almost any product or service could be obtained.

The growing town was huddled in the center of a vast wilderness and was a haven for mountain men and miners. The rugged individuals who carved communities such as Medford, Grants Pass and Klamath Falls from the forests had explored almost every valley and mountain peak by 1870.

CRATER LAKE
1874. FIRST PHOTOGRAM
P. BRITT PHOTO.

Discovered as a result of the exploration of the Oregon Territory that had begun with the first wave of miners and trappers, Crater Lake proved irresistible to Peter Britt. On August 13, 1874, he successfully took his first photograph of the monumental volcanic peak and lake. Twice before, in 1868 and 1869, Britt had journeyed to the brink of the lake to take pictures, but each time foul weather and other factors prevented him from achieving his goal.

CRATERLAKE
Britt
1874

Britt's 1874 expedition was a massive venture and required more than 200 pounds of photographic equipment, including cameras, plates, chemicals and a dark tent. After struggling to the rim, the party spent two days huddled in freezing cold before the weather improved enough to make a picture possible. Britt's photographs set the scene for thousands of other photographers that followed and established him as a pictorialist of national importance.

Peter Britt's epic trip to Crater Lake was only the first of many Britt expeditions to photograph the scenic beauty of Oregon. He journeyed to Rogue River Falls while enroute to the lake. In time, the familiar Britt photographic wagon, which he fondly called "The Pain," had visited hundreds of spots near Jacksonville.

The waters of the Rogue River were a frequent subject for Britt's camera. Because he was on the road for several days at a time and had been left a widower by his wife's death in 1871, his son Emil and daughter Mollie often accompanied him. Both Britt children appear in this scene.

69

With the growth of Jacksonville and the surrounding Rogue River communities, the need for reliable transportation became more apparent. A toll road was established over the Siskiyou Mountains and fees were paid for all that traveled the route. A horse and rider might pay 25 cents and a loaded wagon $1.25, while a single hog cost a mere five cents.

Enroute, travelers would call
upon settler's homes that dotted
the new routes. Typical of many
of the simple frame houses
found in early Oregon was the
Herlineer family dwelling.

In summer, many townspeople would leave home for several months to camp in the cool mountains beside rushing streams. Such camps often grew in number to include scores of people. In popular areas such as those along the Rogue River, small cities of rustic appearance became commonplace.

Camping out was not a sport reserved for the young. Hardy men like Steven Meek, more than 70 years of age when this picture was taken, enjoyed camping beneath the stars as much as the youngsters who accompanied him.

While Jacksonville provided a focal point for the communities surrounding the Rogue River, many settlers barely eked out a living from the rocky soil. Far from friends and neighbors, homesteaders christened their farms with names like Helltown and Riddleburg.

Even these meager homesteads were often located in the midst of incredible beauty. Beyond the Siskiyous, Peter Britt photographed majestic Mount Shasta and visited the lonely outposts scattered beside major routes. His journeys, while short when compared to other practitioners of the time, extended neverthe-less through a region rich with scenic beauty.

Four social organizations linked the citizens of Jacksonville.

Known as the Turnverein, Eintracht, Harmonie and Stamm, the fraternal organizations provided many activities, including concerts, athletic events and picnics.

Outings drew the community together. On occasion, as many as
150 persons would attend such
gatherings. At other times, they
remained intimate reunions with
only the members of a single
family present. After a hearty
meal, children played in the
nearby river while adults engaged in conversation, sang and
strummed musical instruments.

Even Jacksonville was not so remote that it escaped traveling
bands of gypsies plying the roads
between Portland and San Francisco. Stories in the Jacksonville
Reveille occasionally described
the results of their visits — lists
of stolen items or livestock, and
examples of a particular gypsy's
skill at palmistry and fortune-
telling.

The region was also heavily traveled by peddlers selling every possible item of merchandise. Many of the orchards in southern Oregon had their start as seedlings carried overland in wagons filled with pots, glassware, tins of spices and bolts of cloth. Even Peter Britt's prized nursery stock originally came from one such source.

As the demand for housing continued to grow in burgeoning Jacksonville, the Rogue River Valley began to include industry as well as agriculture. Much of the area's lumber came from Henry Lewis' sawmill. Steam power drew the Douglas fir logs through its vertical blades, producing finished planks in a fraction of the time previously required.

Mining with hydraulic water "cannons" soon replaced the lonely placer prospectors and turned many scenic creeks and picturesque rivers into desolate fields of boulders. On occasion, rich strikes would again draw interest to the fields, but Jacksonville increasingly drew its wealth from other sources.

In the earliest years, the Chinese
had provided cheap labor for the
mines. Then, as gold from the
claims dwindled, the Orientals
took them over. To the dismay
of many, abandoned mines often
produced a renewed flow of gold.
The result was a hateful distrust
of the Chinese by many Whites.

Peter Britt seems to have felt much sympathy for the so-called "Celestials." He probably realized early that their successes in the gold mines were more the result of hard work than of secret techniques. In time, Britt took many pictures of the Chinese and seemed to have gained their respect.

Political rallies such as that held for Cleveland in his campaign for the presidency were very popular among Jacksonville's townspeople. On September 28, 1880, President Rutherford B. Hayes and General William T. Sherman made a personal appearance in Jacksonville for one such party. At the fringes of the crowd, President Hayes stopped to shake Emil Britt's hand. For an agonizing moment, Emil stood speechless, but finally managed to sputter out, "Keeno!"

Among Jacksonville's list of
public servants was the Sheriff.
The growing population of the
new state had included ruffians,
con men and desperados, and for
a time the position was a busy
one.

Peter Britt's rustic log cabin, although a sturdy structure that stood amid Britt Park's luxuriant foliage until nearly 1900, proved inadequate as a dwelling just two years after its completion. On his property, Britt erected a series of homes that reflected his ascending position in the community.

A newspaper feature published as a memorial shortly after Peter Britt's death described the Britt grounds' commanding view: "From the north porch of his former house one secures a wonderful view of the historic Rogue River Valley. The porch is a large one, and, of Sunday afternoons years ago, the city band would play and friends of Peter Britt would sit out under the trees and enjoy the music and the cool winds that stole in from the sea to greet the magnolias and the jasmine that bloomed in the yard."

Many of the Swiss-German picnics were massive gatherings that featured every sort of entertainment. The Jacksonville Turnverein afforded social opportunities like many other fraternal groups, but concentrated on physical exercise — including tumbling, gymnastics and building great human pyramids.

Such gatherings frequently were well-lubricated by the flow of wine from Britt's Valley View Vineyards. By 1875, Peter's wine business had grown large enough to attract the attention of the Internal Revenue Service. Although he had recently imported two redwood fermentation tanks capable of holding over 1,000 gallons apiece, he described his enterprise to the government as an overgrown hobby. "The facts are these: I am growing grapes in my garden and make wine in small quantities by natural fermentation and sell occasionally some to my neighbors." Despite his appeal, Britt understandably lost the case.

Because he was a commercial photographer, Britt's collection of Jacksonville pictures reveal every aspect of life in southern Oregon, including the death of some of its residents. Numerous scenes of funeral processions, post mortem portraits and images of grieving survivors remain to mingle with pictures of happier times.

For a short time in the mid-
1870's, pictures such as that
shown below were common.
Grieving widows stood beside
recently-erected tombstones in
these garish photographs. Like
many other tasteless practices,
the popularity of such memorabilia soon ended, but examples
of Britt's efforts to record the
milestones of family life may
still be seen in many albums.

Because Peter Britt drew on his experience as a painter, he often posed his subjects with grace and thought to composition. An ordinary townsman was frequently transformed in the Britt studio as a result of his efforts. Farmers became judges while hard-worked wives returned to youth and beauty.

Portraits recorded every change in social status. Members of a family were often seen to grow from childhood, mature to adults and attain rank and social status before the camera. Officers of lodges and fraternal societies were photographed with the trappings of their newly-won positions. In this manner, Peter Britt's photographs form a remarkable insight into the life of a small western town.

Britt's photographic attentions extended to the members of his own family, who were among the most-photographed citizens of Jacksonville. Any piece of new equipment or new technique for recording images provided occasion for new pictures. While the bulk of these portraits were formally taken, a few captured his children in candid poses such as the one shown above.

The Britt children were given as much schooling as Jacksonville could offer. Jake and Emil attended "Barron" J. L. DeBussche's "Select School," while Mollie boarded at St. Mary's Academy for Young Ladies. St. Mary's was run by Sisters of a Roman Catholic teaching order and was very strict. On one occasion, Mollie was quarantined during Christmas vacation at the school, the result of an infection of measles. Determined to be with her family for the holiday, she opened her second story window, slid down the balcony pole and escaped. The nuns were frantic.

Beside its locally-produced entertainment, Jacksonville frequently hosted traveling companies of players. As individuals, the actors were shunned and their morals questioned, but when the curtain rose performances were usually well attended. The bill of fare ranged in scope from burlesque shows, held in the old thieve's retreat of Kanaka Flats, to Wagnerian operas and melodramatic plays.

Youngsters of the community frequently banded together in cliques and clubs like the "Fan Club" and "Broom Brigade." Part of an era before radio and television, the groups allowed the children to mix socially, often mimicking the antics of their parents' fraternal orders and sewing circles.

Like most studio practitioners, Peter Britt's services included photographing newly-wedded couples. Mr. Colvig and his bride were among those for whom he performed this service, and were photographed on their wedding day, January 23, 1889.

Reputed to be the last of her tribe, Lady Oscharwasha was a Rogue River Indian and often regaled the town youngsters with legends and stories of animals. Even the streams and mountains were living creatures to the first residents of Oregon. Her costume, with its delicately beaded basket hat, was an easy match for the finery heaped on the wedding couples.

99

Because Peter Britt practiced his art for more than 50 years in a single community, he often recorded both travelers and those who lived in the region. Family groups were common, and they often showed several generations of Jacksonville residents.

J. E. Stuart, a prominent landscape painter who traveled the West late in the Nineteenth Century, called upon Peter Britt in Jacksonville and they became close friends. Britt led Stuart to many scenic locales with which the painter was not previously familiar, including Crater Lake, Rogue River Falls and Lake of the Woods.

During the 1880's, photographs of people in costumes became popular and studios bristled with pictures of "Indian scouts," "frontiersmen" and "pilgrims." With the passage of time, individuals who had actually followed the trails West and settled the wilderness dwindled. Instead, their children and grandchildren romanticized the colonial and frontier period.

Much of these costumed photographs' popularity was a result of the Centennial celebration of 1876. Fourth of July festivities grew to an importance that they had not enjoyed since before the Civil War years. Coupled with the move toward costumes and fantasy, the patriotic Oregonians dressed their children as Martha and George Washington, Patrick Henry, John Paul Jones and Abigail Adams.

As ever, Peter Britt's camera photographed the truth of his subject's appearances. Although Britt might, through delicate posing, studio props or fanciful backdrops, embue his client with grace or expression, the reality of their features remained beyond artistic tampering. The fair were portrayed as lovely, and the plain perhaps more so.

Family groups such as that
above must have driven the ide-
alistic Britt to distraction. Six
daughters — and each without
much hope of marriage. Perhaps
it was the members of this family
that prompted Britt's outburst
to one sitter, "Miss, if you want
a beautiful face, you must bring
one with you!"

By the year 1900, when Peter Britt at last put his camera aside, his children were grown. Emil had taken his place, first at Peter's side and later as a photographer in his own right. Mollie, who as a young girl had made ice cream from late-season mountain snow in a scheme to buy a new carpet for the parlor, was now the mistress of the Britt house. Britt's stark pioneer existance had been replaced with successful opulence.

Plate Credits

Page 30 (lower) courtesy Peter E. Palmquist. Page 52 courtesy International Museum of Photography at George Eastman House. All other photographs courtesy Southern Oregon Historical Society and the Jacksonville Museum. Illustrations pages 19, 21, 22, 24, 25, 30 and 33 courtesy Jere Smith.